I AM THE

Chrissy Williams lives in southeast London and edits PERVERSE magazine.

Also by Chrissy Williams

Low	(Bloodaxe Books, 2021)
Bear	(Bloodaxe Books, 2017)
This	(If a Leaf Falls Press, 2016)
Seven Poems	(Happenstance Press, 2014)
Epigraphs	(If P Then Q, 2014)
Flying into the Bear	(Happenstance Press, 2013)
The Jam Trap	(Soaring Penguin, 2012)

I am the Table:
Poems found on *Love Island*

Chrissy Williams

ISBN: 978-1-915079-92-3

Cover designed by Aaron Kent

Edited and typeset by Aaron Kent

Broken Sleep Books Ltd
Rhydwen,
Talgarreg,
Ceredigion,
SA44 4HB

Broken Sleep Books Ltd
Fair View,
St Georges Road
Cornwall
PL26 7YH

Contents

"My purpose was... to adopt the very language of men..."

> — William Wordsworth

I want someone
I can just
be myself around

♥

I want someone
who will literally
tear me a new arsehole

♥

I want a relationship
that lasts more than
eight weeks

♥

I like a bold
pubic
region

♥

I like a big
like a gym
like a big gym goer

♥

I'm going to see
if I can squeeze a bit
of life out of him

He's so funny
so funny
like, not quick-witted
but so funny

♥

A lot of people
spend a lot of time
overthinking things
but she doesn't do that

♥

I don't want to have kids
with someone where I feel
like I'm doing everything

♥

One of your hairs
is on my pastries

♥

There's a few little red flags popped up
in the last couple of days but
they're only *little* red flags, so

♥

It doesn't make
any sense
at all

Did I
jump in
too quickly?

♥

Oh mate I'm calm
I'm calm I'm calm
I'm calm

♥

Ugh
cats

♥

Missionary?
That's boring
like eating a cracker
without butter

♥

I don't do that
I'm not that girl
I won't laugh at you
to make your dick feel bigger

♥

He wanted to blindside me
with shitty personal comments
for me the whole thing
feels like a shitty cheap shot

I don't do
fiery girls

♥

You're
a strong
woman

♥

I think
I literally was
a placeholder
blue-tacked to
someone else

♥

I'm not going to lie
this tastes
really fucking weird

♥

There's a new girl
coming in and she could
fuck shit up

♥

I already
knew
you'd be
annoyed

I think
she'd be fine with it
it tests me
and it tests her

♥

If I fall at this hurdle
it's not worth continuing
because the outside world
will be twenty times worse

♥

Get on
with your conversation
and I'm gonna get on
with mine

♥

I want to get to know her
and see what she's about

♥

We may or may not
have snogged on the terrace
It was an accident

♥

She gave in
She gave in
She gave in

I'm a try
before you buy
kinda girl

♥

You shouldn't need
to do the orgasm on your own
It should be a joint effort

♥

It wouldn't be the first time
he's not stood up
and been a man about something

♥

Good things come
to those who wait

♥

What more do you want from a day?
You stink
but you got a kiss

♥

I walked into
a lions' den and
ruffled
some feathers

I wanted to
knock you down
a peg or two

♥

My response was
"I don't regret it"
which is completely the wrong response you can ever say

♥

I'm learning
I don't know what to do
I don't know how to talk to girls

♥

I'm really looking forward to
continuing to get to know you
even though you are a pain in my arse
both cheeks

♥

I thought I was going like a tortoise
but they're making me look like a snail's pace

♥

It's either gonna make us
or break us
and at the moment
it looks like it's breaking

Traps are everywhere
Traps
Traps
Traps
Traps
Traps

♥

You'll always
be the tallest
in my eyes

♥

I firmly believe that
a lot of this test stuff
is total bullshit

♥

How much have you got to learn?
How many mistakes have you gotta make?

♥

I've almost got to
pull my finger out
and actually understand
where my head is at

♥

I don't think
I even like sport
any more

Honestly in this place
you have to be brave
you have to be bold
you have to take risks

♥

Let's
go
eat
sweets

♥

I will get myself
balls deep
in any situation

♥

Chirpse
chirpse
graft
graft

♥

I'll be whatever
you want me to be
right, come on

♥

Job done.

.

"Job done?"

♥

Jesus
What is this?

♥

That was
really nice
loved it
thanks

♥

It's just little things
I want a cuddle, a kiss
just having a laugh, having a chat
about how long's that tree been there for
just general stuff

♥

I wanna live life without regrets
but I gotta say
that was a regret

♥

How many lessons
does one man need?

♥

I am a bad person
I can't keep doing this

I am mature enough
to understand
everything
that's going on here

♥

We were in
the same situation
We acted
differently

♥

I don't feel like I deserve
someone to realise
how much they like me
by getting to know someone else
and kissing them

♥

When you know
you know
and you don't need
someone else
to confirm it

♥

No
How many lessons
does one guy need
seriously

I don't know why to say
I don't know what to do
It's getting out of control
I'm just... fuck

♥

I've fucked it
I've fucked it
big time
I'm a bad person
It's just...
You can't keep doing this shit

♥

I'm having
deep thoughts here
and you guys
are laughing

♥

When am I not
in a bit of a pickle?
I'm always in
a bit of a pickle

♥

You may need to reassess
whether or not it's annoying you
if it's just a bit of jealousy
or whether it's actually annoying you
because you could be doing
the same thing

20

This is uncharted territory for me
I don't know *what* the fuck I'm doing
I'm just acting off emotions

♥

I'm mad chill right now
but I don't know
I could switch very easily

♥

That was cute
not enough
but cute

♥

Let's carry on
being strong

♥

I don't think
he'll fit in with my family
He's so kind and such a lovely person
and we are brutal
Maybe I'm not
good enough
for him

♥

I'm so proud of you
you've blossomed
into a man

It's like
a relationship
crash course
in five weeks

♥

I need to stop worrying about the future
that hasn't happened yet
and just be here in the present with you now

♥

He's basically telling the guys
to throw their Twix
down a fucking alleyway

♥

All I've ever done
is give people advice
and opinions

♥

She's going to keep
pushing and pushing
people away

♥

I will fall out
with every single
prick in this place

Sexually attractive
sexual connection
potato po*ta*to

♥

I'm no master but
I've literally been through
every single mistake in this villa
and don't want her to make
the same mistakes I have

♥

I don't want to be the one again
to let myself ruin
something good for myself

♥

You know
she likes to shout, bro

♥

I just want to listen
to what she wants to say

♥

I'd rather be done
than be hurt

Don't always think
that it's just down to you

♥

We can take the load as well with you
We can take the load with you

♥

Worry leads to wrinkles
wrinkles lead to Botox
and more Botox means
potentially my face
will drop

♥

Are you
fucking serious
I'm a weapon

♥

I never think about future me
Actually I sabotage her every day
just by being a nob

♥

You know
when you're on a rollercoaster
and it does that drop
it's like that
it's not nice

This is the first time in life
I've not been able to run
and it's scary

♥

Let's see
how today
goes

♥

That's what makes me think
what's for the cameras
what's not for the cameras
what's genuine
what's not genuine

♥

I know you keep saying
remember we're on a TV show
but what makes it good
is being yourself

♥

I know
what I bring to the table
I am
the fucking table
with the fruit on

He had
the confidence
of the Prime Minister

♥

It's not like
you can fake
something like that
for this amount of time

♥

You know what
no risk
no reward

♥

Shoulders?
Back?
Feet?

♥

Sometimes you gotta
push it to the side
enjoy yourselves again
come back at it from a different angle

♥

Take no shit
Take no mercy

I'm sick
of this toxic masculinity
take me out
I want to be treated
like a princess

Everyone's entitled to their own opinion
I don't care
She cares about people's opinions

It's about time people said things
how they're really feeling

I feel like
this garlic bread
almost
represents me

He says he loves me
but he doesn't
those are just words
it's not what he does

I don't think he's a bad person
he just wasn't in love with me
and that's okay

Acknowledgements

With thanks to the cast of Love Island 2021.

COUPLE UP WITH YOUR UNREST